The Halloween Activity Book

Creepy, Crawly, Hairy, Scary Things to Do

By Mymi Doinet

Illustrated by Benjamin Chaud

chronicle books · san francisco

First published in the United States in 2002 by Chronicle Books LLC.

Copyright © 2001 by Nathan/VUEF (Paris-France).

English text and translation © 2002 by Chronicle Books.

Originally published in France in 2000 by Editions Nathan/HER (Paris-France).

All rights reserved.

English type design by Jessica Dacher.

Typeset in Duckweed, Randumhouse, and Zemke Hand.

The illustrations in this book were rendered in gouache and ink.

Manufactured in China.

Library of Congress Cataloging-in-Publication Data

Doinet, Mymi.

The Halloween activity book : creepy, crawly, hairy, scary things to do / Mymi Doinet, Benjamin Chaud.

p. cm.

Summary: Suggests a variety of activities related to Halloween,
including making costumes, decorations, invitation cards, and snacks.

ISBN 0-8118-3279-1

1. Halloween decorations-Juvenile literature.

2. Handicraft-Juvenile literature. [1. Halloween. 2. Costume. 3. Halloween decorations. 4. Handicraft.]

I. Chaud, Benjamin. II. Title.

TT900.H32 D65 2002

745.594'1646—dc21

2001005823

Distributed in Canada by Raincoast Books

9050 Shaughnessy Street, Vancouver, British Columbia V6P 6E5

10 9 8 7 6 5 4 3 2 1

Chronicle Books LLC

85 Second Street, San Francisco, California 94105

www.chroniclekids.com

CONTENTS

How Halloween Started

A Spooky New Year's Eve Party

Two thousand years ago, the Celtic people of England, Ireland, and northern France started their new year on November 1, which marked the end of the harvest and the beginning of the dark winter months. On the last night of October, they gathered to celebrate their New Year's Eve festival. They lit huge bonfires, which would help make the short days of the coming winter seem longer. They also wore scary masks to frighten away the ghosts and goblins that were thought to walk the earth on that night, causing trouble.

Halloween in America

Lots of Celtic people moved to the United States and they brought their customs with them. Since the nineteenth century, Halloween has been celebrated all across the country.

"Trick or Treat!"

According to the Celts, the spirits that came out on Halloween would disguise themselves and knock on doors, asking for food or little presents. If the people who answered the doors didn't give out treats, the spirits would play pranks on them. This is one of the origins of our modern custom of trick-or-treating.

The Legend of Jack and His Lantern

The story of Jack-o'-Lantern is an old Irish one. Jack was a stingy man who spent all his time drinking. When he died, God wouldn't let him into heaven. So Jack used a glowing ember, which he carried in a hollow turnip, to light his way back to earth. People who knew the story started using "Jack's lanterns" to scare away the spirits of Halloween. When Celtic people came to the United States, they found that pumpkins worked even better than turnips for lanterns, and that's how we started carving pumpkins for jack-o'-lanterns.

Witch Wardrobe

Mirror, mirror on the wall,
what's the best Halloween costume of all?
A witch, of course!
(Ghosts and vampires are good too;
we'll get to those soon.)

Creepy Clothes

Dress in a long-sleeved black T-shirt, a long black skirt, and black shoes. Throw a piece of black cloth over your shoulders, like a shawl. Cut the fingertips off a pair of black gloves so your fingers will stick out. (Make sure your parents say it's okay!) If you want to, polish your fingernails black or wear long black stick-on nails.

Horrifying Hat

1. Cut a quarter of a circle with an 18-inch radius from a big sheet of black construction paper. Tape the straight edges together to make a cone. Make sure the base of the cone is even, so the cone stands up straight.

2. Cut a circle with a 14-inch diameter from black construction paper. Place the cone in the middle of the circle and trace the cone's base with a pencil or chalk. Then cut along your line to make a round hole in the middle of the circle.

3. Cut several ½-inch notches around the base of the cone, then fold the tabs under the circle and tape them down. If you like, wind a rubber snake around the brim of the hat or attach plastic spiders to your hair with bobby pins.

18"

14"

6

Mysterious Makeup

Apply a layer of white or green makeup to your face—or use both.

Color your lips with black or green lipstick.

Use a black makeup pencil to darken your eyebrows. Smudge black makeup under your eyes.

Draw some warts on your face with a brown makeup pencil.

Spooky Spell Book

To make a book where you keep your most powerful spells, start with a blank notebook. Cut 2 pieces of cardboard slightly wider than the notebook and glue them to the front and back covers. Punch a hole in the edge of both the front and back covers, and tie a string to each hole. Tie the strings together to close the spell book. Decorate the front cover with charms and warnings and a picture of something scary, like a snake.

Ghost Gear

A ghost is one of the easiest costumes you can make. All you really need is a sheet, some white clothes, and a horrible, hollow moan.

1. Ask an adult to cut a circle with a 5- to 7-foot diameter in an old white sheet (the size depends on your height). Drape the circle over your head and have an adult mark on the sheet where your eyes are.

2. Take off the sheet and cut 2 small holes where the marks were made.

3. Slip the sheet on over white pants, white socks and tennis shoes, a long-sleeved white T-shirt, and white gloves. You are now dressed to chill!

4. A well-dressed ghost never goes out without a ball and chain. To make one, tie a 2-foot piece of plastic chain to a black ball of yarn (put some dark rubber bands around the yarn so it doesn't unravel). Then tie the chain to one of your ankles.

8

Undead Threads
(Or, How to Dress Like a Vampire)

Sinister Suit

Dress in black pants, black shoes, black socks, and a white buttoned shirt.

Frightening Face

Apply a layer of white makeup to your face. Draw on thick black eyebrows with a black makeup pencil. Color your lips with blood-red lipstick. Put in a pair of plastic fangs. Add a bit of red lipstick to the tips of your fangs for an extra-creepy effect.

Creepy Cape

Use a piece of black cloth 4 to 6 feet wide and 2 to 4 feet long, depending on your height. Ask an adult to sew a 2-inch hem on one of the short ends. Thread a 4-foot-long piece of black cord through the hem and tie the ends around your neck. Totally terrifying!

How Does Your Pumpkin Grow?

Did you know you can grow your own pumpkins for Halloween? But beware! You have to plant them in May (after the last frost) if you want them to be nice and round by fall.

1. Soak pumpkin seeds in a bowl of water for 24 hours. Fill several clay flower pots with potting soil. Bury 2 seeds in each pot, about ½ inch deep.

2. Put the pots near a window where they will get direct sunlight. Water them every 2 days. After about 15 days, little plants will appear.

3. In your garden, dig holes that are about 9 inches across, 9 inches deep, and 3 feet apart. Gently replant the seedlings in the holes. Pretty soon, yellow blossoms will appear. The first ones will usually fall off—that's okay! The next ones will stay and grow into pumpkins.

4. In the hot summertime, water the plants daily, either early in the morning or in the evening. Make sure the soil never stays dry for long. As the pumpkins grow, gently turn them over once or twice so they don't get flat on the side that rests on the ground.

5. By the end of September, the pumpkins will be orange and ripe. Pick them before it begins to get cold, and store them in a cool, dark place until Halloween.

Jack-o'-Lanterns

Turning ordinary pumpkins into spooky jack-o'-lanterns takes strong magic, but you will need an adult to help with the fire.

1. [Cover] your work surface [with newspaper]. Ask [a grown-up to] cut out the [top of the pumpkin.]

2. Scoop out the pumpkin seeds and stringy stuff with your hands or a spoon, until the inside of the pumpkin is clean and smooth. Save the seeds in a bowl.

3. With a washable marker, draw a face on the pumpkin. Ask a grown-up to help carve out the eyes, nose, and mouth.

4. Set a candle inside the pumpkin and put the top on. Put it on your porch or front steps, or in a window. When night comes, it's time to light the candle.

Sorcerer's Seeds

Soak the seeds from your pumpkin until they're clean. Spread them out to dry, then lay them on a baking sheet and sprinkle a little vegetable oil over them. With an adult's help, toast the seeds for 10 to 15 minutes in an oven preheated to 325°F, stirring once or twice so they brown evenly. When they're brown, take them out, sprinkle salt on them, let them [cool, then] snack away!

The Witch's Den

Having some friends over to howl at the moon?
Here are some ways to prepare your lair.

Door of Doom

You will need
Double-sided tape
Several big sheets of black
  construction paper
Purple crepe paper
Green rubber gloves
Black yarn
Witch or monster mask
Broom (optional)
Glue

1. Using the double-sided tape, cover a door with the black construction paper. Cut the purple crepe paper into long streamers and tape several of them to either side of the door, like curtains.

2. Tape the gloves across the curtains. (It should look like the hands are coming around the sides of the door and holding back the curtains.) Using the black yarn, hang the mask from the top of the door. If your mask is a witch, prop the broom in one of the gloves.

You will need
Pale green balloons
Black permanent marker
Glue
Black yarn
Plastic spiders

1. Blow up the balloons and tie their ends.

2. With the marker, draw zombie or witch faces on the balloons, being careful not to smear the ink.

3. Glue pieces of black yarn to the heads for hair and attach the plastic spiders to the hair.

4. Hang the heads up all around the room.

Monster Mirror

You will need

Tape
Aluminum foil
2 pieces of 12-by-16-inch
  poster board
Pencil
Scissors
Paintbrush
Black and green water-based paint
Glitter
Clear glue
White paper

1. Tape a sheet of aluminum foil to 1 piece of poster board with the shiny side facing out to make the mirror.

2. With the pencil, draw a rectangle 2 inches inside the edges of the second piece of poster board. Cut out the smaller rectangle to make a frame. Paint the frame black, glue some glitter on it, and glue it onto the mirror.

3. On the white paper, trace or draw 4 copies of one of the toads on page 17. Cut them out and paint them green. Glue some glitter on their eyes, then glue one toad to each corner of the mirror.

4. Ask your parents to help you hang the mirror on the front door so your friends can see how gross they look.

Spiderweb Windows

You will need

8 wood skewers
Ball of white string
Newspaper
Black spray paint
Glue
4 plastic spiders

1. To make each spiderweb, arrange 2 skewers in a cross shape and wind the string around and around the center until the skewers stay put.

2. Start winding the string between the arms of the cross, leaving space between the strands, to make a spiderweb.

3. Do the same thing with the other skewers until you have 4 spiderwebs.

4. Put the spiderwebs on sheets of newspaper and have a grown-up paint them on both sides with the black spray paint. Let them dry.

5. Glue a spider to the middle of each spiderweb and hang them in your windows.

Ghastly Garlands

Make lots of these to transform your house into a haunted mansion.

5"

You will need
Orange, white, and black tissue paper
Paper clips
Pencil
Scissors
Black felt-tip pen

1. Cut several strips of tissue paper 5 inches wide and 2 to 3 feet long.

2. Fold the strips every 4 inches in an accordion shape. Use 2 paper clips to hold the folds together.

3. Using the pencil, outline pumpkin shapes on the first layer of orange tissue paper, ghosts on the white tissue paper, and bats on the black paper.

4. Cut through all the layers of paper at once, following the outlines you drew.

5. Unfold the garlands. If you like, draw faces on the pumpkins and eyes on the ghosts with the felt-tip pen.

Frightful Invites

You will need

White, black, and orange construction paper
Pencil
Craft knife
Clear glue
4-by-6-inch envelopes
Halloween stickers
Tape
Can of spray snow

1. Draw the shapes above on some of the construction paper. Make big ones (as big as your paper) to put in the window and smaller ones (about 3 by 4 inches) to put on the invitations. Hint: if you are making more than 2 or 3 invitations, draw 1, cut it out, and trace around it to draw the others.

2. Ask an adult to cut out the shapes with the craft knife.

3. To make the invitations, fold 5-by-7-inch rectangles of construction paper in half (this will make cards that are 3½ by 5 inches). Glue different-colored cutouts onto the cards (put orange pumpkins on black cards, for instance). Write the details of your party inside each invitation, put them in the envelopes, and seal with the stickers.

4. Tape the bigger cutouts to your windowpanes and spray them with the fake snow. (In this case, the white stuff in the can is not snow, but eerie fog rising from the graveyard.)

Setting the Sorcerer's Table

Before you serve your favorite dishes—snake stew and fried bat brains—make your table look as fearsome as can be!

Pumpkin and cauldron Place mats

You will need

1 piece of 12-by-14-inch poster board for each guest

Pencil

Scissors

Black, orange, and gold water-based paint

Paintbrush

Plastic lamination rolls or sheets

1. To create a place mat for each guest, draw a pumpkin or cauldron on each piece of poster board, then have an adult cut them out.

2. Paint the pumpkins orange with black noses, mouths, and eyes. Paint the cauldrons black with gold handles.

3. When the place mats are dry, cover them on each side with lamination. Trim the extra lamination from the edges.

Toad Tableware

You will need

Several sheets of green paper
Pencil
Dark green and purple markers
Scissors
Clear glue
Clear plastic plates
Clear plastic cups
Clear plastic pitcher

1. Draw the toads at left onto the green paper. Make 1 to 3 toads for each plate or cup, and 4 to 5 more for the pitcher.

2. Draw green warts and purple eyes on the toads with the markers, then cut them out.

3. To make the plates, spread a thin layer of glue on the top of each toad. Stick them carefully to the bottoms of the plates.

4. To make the cups and pitcher, spread glue on the bottom of the toads. Stick them to the outsides of the cups and pitcher.

Scary Straws

You will need

1 big sheet of white construction paper
Colored markers
Scissors
Tape
Bendy straws

1. On the construction paper, draw, color, and cut out small pumpkins, ghosts, skulls, and black cats.

2. Tape 1 cutout to each straw.

Cold Ghost Blood

What color is ghost blood? No color at all! Pour clear soda into tall glasses with ice, and serve with Scary Straws.

The Witch's Diner

Witches are always cooking up something vile. Here are enough witchy treats for six horribly hungry kids.

Snake Guts

You will need

3 ripe avocados
Bowl
3 tablespoons tomato salsa
Pinch of salt
1 teaspoon lemon juice
1 cucumber, sliced
Tortilla chips

1. Peel the avocados and remove their pits. Mash the avocado in the bowl with a fork.
2. Mix in the salsa, salt, and lemon juice.
3. Place the cucumber slices around the rim of the bowl, then spoon in the avocado mixture.
4. Serve with the tortilla chips.

Spider Pizza

You will need

1 prebaked pizza crust, or package
   of premade pizza dough
½ jar pizza sauce
1½ cups grated mozzarella cheese
½ cup ricotta cheese
1 tablespoon milk
Green and red food coloring
Plastic squeeze bottle
1 plastic spider

1. Ask an adult to preheat the oven according to the directions on
   the pizza crust or dough package.

2. Lay the pizza crust or dough on a baking sheet. Spread the pizza sauce
   on it and sprinkle the mozzarella cheese evenly over the top.

3. With an adult's help, bake the pizza according to the package directions.

4. While the pizza is baking, mix together the ricotta cheese, milk, 6 drops of green
   food coloring, and 1 drop of red food coloring. Spoon the mixture into the
   squeeze bottle.

5. When the pizza is baked, remove it from the oven. Draw a spiderweb on the pizza
   with the ricotta mixture in the squeeze bottle. Place the plastic spider in the
   middle of the spiderweb and serve.

Giant Tarantulas

You will need

24 brown or black pipe cleaners or thin
   licorice ropes cut into 24 pieces
6 chocolate-frosted chocolate cupcakes
12 red cinnamon candies

1. If using pipe cleaners, cut each pipe cleaner
   in half. Stick 8 pipe cleaner pieces or 8
   lengths of licorice into each of the cupcakes
   so they look like long tarantula legs.

2. Stick 2 cinnamon candies close together
   between each spider's front legs to make
   the tarantula's beady red eyes.

Vampire Snack Bar

One thing we know about vampires—
they love to eat. If one or two are coming
to your party, be prepared with these gory
treats. All these recipes make enough for
six little bloodsuckers.

Flesh Kabobs

You will need
2 pints cherry tomatoes
6 hot dogs
6 rolls string cheese
2 cucumbers
6 wood skewers

1. Wash the cherry tomatoes and take off their stems.
   Ask an adult to cook the hot dogs for 7 minutes in
   simmering water.

2. Cut the hot dogs, string cheese, and cucumbers
   into ½-inch slices.

3. Slide a cherry tomato onto a skewer, then a slice of
   hot dog, then a slice of string cheese, then a slice
   of cucumber, then a tomato... and so on
   until all the skewers are full. Serve.

Bat Burgers

You will need

Tape
6 little cut-out bats
6 toothpicks
6 cooked hamburger patties
6 hamburger buns
Ketchup and whatever else you
   like on hamburgers

1. Tape the bats to the toothpicks. Put the hamburgers in their buns and stick a bat-pick into each top bun.

2. Serve with ketchup and burger fixings.

Blood Cocktails

Just what a thirsty vampire loves to suck down! Pour 2 tablespoons of grenadine or strawberry syrup into each of 6 tall glasses. Add some ice and lemon-lime soda, and serve with Scary Straws (page 17).

Killer Chiller Sundaes

You will need

1 quart of vanilla ice cream
1 pint of fresh strawberries, stemmed and sliced
Strawberry syrup

1. Scoop ice cream into 6 dishes and scatter strawberry slices on top.

2. Pour strawberry syrup on each sundae. When your guests ask what that red stuff is, just laugh an evil vampire laugh.

Pumpkin Potion

This pumpkin butter tastes magical on your morning toast. Your parents can help you seal it in jars to make a ghoulishly good party favor.

You will need

1 cup dried apricots
1 can (15 ounces) solid pumpkin pack
²/₃ cup firmly packed brown sugar
2 teaspoons lemon juice
¹/₂ teaspoon ground cinnamon
6 canning jars (4 ounces) with 2-piece lids
Glue
6 plastic spiders
Labels
Colored markers

1. Soak the dried apricots overnight in a bowl of lukewarm water. The next day, drain them and have an adult mince them into tiny pieces.

2. Mix the apricots, pumpkin, sugar, lemon juice, and cinnamon in a saucepan. With an adult, bring to a boil over medium-high heat, stirring often. Reduce the heat to medium-low and simmer for 20 minutes, stirring occasionally. While the potion is cooking, ask a grown-up to sterilize the jars and their lids in boiling water.

3. Take the mixture off the heat and spoon it immediately into the sterilized jars. Seal the lids tightly on the jars, then ask a grown-up to boil them in water for 15 more minutes.

4. When the jars are cool, glue a plastic spider to the top of each jar. Make a label for each jar with the markers. Write "Pumpkin Potion" and be sure to include the date. The potion will last 2 months unopened and 2 weeks in the refrigerator after it's opened.

Boo Cookies

Boo Cookies are frightfully delicious.
This recipe makes twelve.

You will need
1 cup powdered sugar
1 cup butter or margarine
2 eggs
2 teaspoons vanilla
3 cups flour
1 teaspoon baking soda
1 teaspoon cream of tartar
White and black icing

1. Combine the sugar, butter or margarine, eggs, and vanilla in a large mixing bowl. In another bowl, combine the flour, baking soda, and cream of tartar. Gradually mix the dry ingredients into the wet ingredients.

2. Cover and refrigerate the dough for 2 hours.

3. Ask an adult to preheat the oven to 375°F. Roll out the dough on a lightly floured surface until it's ¼ inch thick.

4. Cut the dough into ghost shapes and place them on a lightly greased baking sheet. With an adult's help, bake for 8 minutes, or until the edges start to brown.

5. After the cookies have cooled, decorate with the white icing. Draw eyes and mouths with the black icing.

Baby Boas

Make the dough for the Boo Cookies and set aside 1 tablespoon of it. Mix 8 drops of green food coloring into the large portion of dough. Mix 1 drop of red food coloring into the tablespoon that was set aside. Refrigerate the dough for 2 hours. Roll pieces of the green dough into cylinders about ½ inch thick and 4 inches long. Make little cuts in one end for the snakes' mouths. Roll little bits of the pink dough into balls and press them into the dough above the snakes' mouths to make the eyes. Set the boas on a lightly greased baking sheet. Bake in an oven preheated to 375°F, for 10 minutes. To serve, arrange the boas on a platter, and put little pieces of black licorice in their mouths for tongues.

Chocolate Midnight Witch Cake

If you thought devil's food cake was good, wait until you try this!

You will need

3 eggs

²/₃ cup granulated sugar

¹/₄ cup plus 1 tablespoon flour

¹/₄ cup plus 1 tablespoon cornstarch

2 teaspoons baking powder

¹/₃ cup butter

7 ounces semisweet chocolate chips

2 bananas

Tracing paper

Pencil

Confectioners' sugar

1. Ask an adult to preheat the oven to 425°F.

2. Beat together the eggs and the granulated sugar in a bowl. Mix in the flour, cornstarch, and baking powder.

3. With an adult, melt the butter and chocolate in the top of a double boiler.

4. Peel the bananas and mash them with a fork. Add the bananas, melted chocolate, and butter to the other ingredients and mix well.

5. Pour the mixture into a greased 9-inch round cake pan. Bake for 35 minutes.

6. After removing it from the oven, let the cake cool. Then remove it from the cake pan onto a big plate.

7. Trace the witch and her broom, stars, and bat from this page onto a sheet of tracing paper. Ask an adult to cut out the shapes with a craft knife. Place the tracing paper over the cake and sift confectioners' sugar over the top. Gently remove the paper and kazam—Chocolate Midnight Witch Cake!

Haunted Houses

Gingerbread houses make the perfect haunts, but beware! They take two days to make.

You will need

Batch of gingerbread cookie dough
2 egg whites
½ teaspoon cream of tartar
2 cups confectioners' sugar
2 pieces of sturdy 1-foot-square cardboard
Icing in various colors
Sugar ice-cream cones
Various colorful hard candies
Gummy creatures—the grossest ones you can find

1. Roll out the dough on a lightly floured surface until it's ¼ inch thick. With help, cut the dough into house shapes: two 5-by-8-inch rectangles for the side walls, two 6-by-10-inch rectangles for the roof, and two 5-by-9-inch pointed end pieces, with the pointed sides starting 5 inches from the bottom.

2. Bake on a lightly greased cookie sheet in an oven preheated to 350°F, for 10 to 12 minutes. Trim the pieces when they're still warm to make sure they're even.

3. To create the icing you'll use to "glue" the house together, beat together the egg whites and cream of tartar until stiff peaks form. Mix in the confectioners' sugar.

4. Assembling the house might require the help of an accomplice. Draw an L shape with the icing "glue" on a piece of cardboard. Stand a side wall and a pointed end piece on the icing and use more icing to affix them together where they touch. Carefully hold the walls until the icing hardens, about 15 minutes. Use icing to hold the other 2 walls in place and let dry for 1 hour. "Glue" the roof pieces on, holding them in place until secure. Leave overnight to harden.

5. The next day, decorate! With the colored icing, stick on the ice-cream cones for turrets, draw doors and windows, and stick candies all over the walls and roof. Put the gross gummy creatures around the house to guard it.

Nightmare Theater

You will need

1 big cardboard box

Scissors

Tape

Pencil

1 big sheet of tracing paper,
   almost as big as the box's bottom

Black construction paper

Glue stick

Craft knife

Wood skewers

Lamp

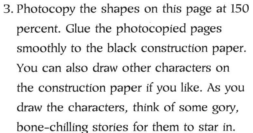

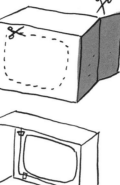

1. Remove the cardboard flaps from the top of the box and remove the 2 smaller flaps from the bottom of the box. Tape the 2 remaining flaps together at both ends, then cut a rectangle out of it to create a "window."

2. Tape the tracing paper over the "window" on the inside of the box.

3. Photocopy the shapes on this page at 150 percent. Glue the photocopied pages smoothly to the black construction paper. You can also draw other characters on the construction paper if you like. As you draw the characters, think of some gory, bone-chilling stories for them to star in.

4. Ask an adult to cut out the shapes with the craft knife. Tape a skewer to the back of each of shape.

5. Set the box on a table and put the lamp behind it (take off the lamp's shade if it has one). Invite all your friends to sit in front of the theater. Turn off the lights and light the lamp. Let the show begin!

Truth or Scare Darts

You will need
White board or blackboard
Dry-erase pens or chalk
Rubber-tipped darts
Big bag of candy
Paper and pencil
Apples

1. Draw a little pumpkin shape in the middle of the board. (Use dry-erase pens on the white board or chalk on the blackboard.) Write the number 1 in the middle of the little pumpkin.

2. Draw 4 bigger pumpkins around the little pumpkin and number them 2 through 5 (see illustration). Color in the pumpkins. Draw a stem at the top of the biggest pumpkin shape.

3. Take turns throwing darts at the board. The number you hit corresponds to a prize, a dare, or a truth (see page 29).

4. The darts may rub off some of the pattern, so touch up the lines of the pumpkins as you play.

Your fate depends upon where your dart lands, so beware! If you don't hit a number, you have to perform a dare proposed by the other players.

1. Bullseye! Reach into the bag for a handful of candy.
2. Bite an apple with your hands tied behind your back.
3. Write your first and last name with your left hand if you are right-handed, or vice versa.
4. Draw a spider and its web in less than 2 minutes.
5. Truthfully answer any question your friends ask.

Double Jeopardy

Luck, memory, and psychic powers
will get you far in this card game.

To make the cards

Photocopy these 2 pages at 150 percent and cut the pictures out along the dotted lines. Glue or tape the pictures to the fronts of old playing cards or to pieces of cardboard. If you like, color the pictures with crayons or markers.

To play the game

1. Two or more people can play. Shuffle the cards well and spread them out facedown on a table.

2. Each player turns over 2 cards, one after the other. If the upturned cards are the same, the player keeps the pair of cards and plays again. If the upturned cards are different, the player replaces them facedown.

3. When there are no more card left facedown, count your cards. The player with the most cards wins.

Evil Eye and Crypt

These are two good games to play if
you have a gaggle of goblins.

To play Evil Eye, take as many playing
cards from a deck as there are players.
Decide which card is the evil-eye card,
then shuffle the cards. Each player picks
a card and doesn't show it. All the players
sit in a circle and look at each other. The
player with the evil eye winks at another
player. That person waits 5 seconds, then
falls over "dead." If another player knows
who has the evil eye, that player points
and says, "You have the evil eye." If
wrong, both players are dead. If right,
that player wins. If the player with the
evil eye gets everyone, consider it a
victory.

In Crypt, one person (the
corpse) goes to hide while the
others cover their eyes and count to
50. Then everyone starts looking for the
corpse. Each player that finds the corpse
has to hide with the corpse in the crypt.
When only 1 person is left outside the
crypt, the game is over. The first person to
find the corpse gets to be the corpse in
the next round.